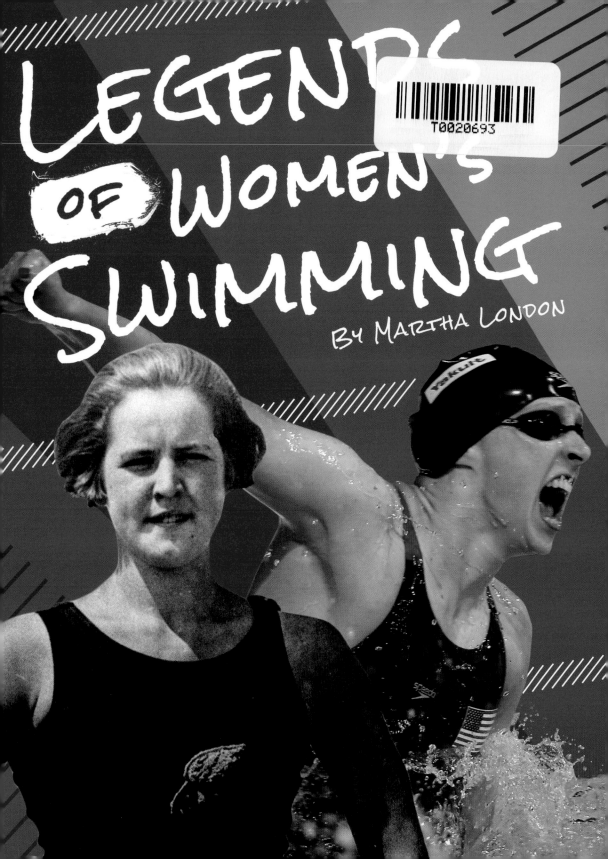

LEGENDS
OF WOMEN'S
SWIMMING

BY MARTHA LONDON

T0020693

Book design by Sarah Taplin
Cover design by Sarah Taplin

Photographs ©: AP Images, cover (left), 1 (left), 8, 11, 18; Daniel Ochoa de Olza/AP Images, cover (right), 1 (right); Shutterstock Images, 4, 24, 27; ullstein bild/Getty Images, 7; Bettmann/Getty Images, 12; Jon Super/AP Images, 15; J Pat Carter/AP Images, 16; Mark J. Terrill/AP Images, 20; Lennox McLendon/AP Images, 22; Kirsty Wigglesworth/AP Images, 29

Press Box Books, an imprint of Press Room Editions.

ISBN
978-1-63494-285-0 (library bound)
978-1-63494-303-1 (paperback)
978-1-63494-339-0 (epub)
978-1-63494-321-5 (hosted ebook)

Library of Congress Control Number: 2020913874

Distributed by North Star Editions, Inc.
2297 Waters Drive
Mendota Heights, MN 55120
www.northstareditions.com

Printed in the United States of America
012021

About the Author
Martha London works full-time writing children's books. When she isn't writing, you can find her hiking in the woods.

TABLE OF CONTENTS

CHAPTER 1

MAKING WAVES

All eyes were on Katie Ledecky. The US swimmer inched ahead stroke by stroke. With each lap, her lead grew. As she neared the end of the 800-meter freestyle at the 2016 Olympics in Brazil, Ledecky surged forward. Her hands touched the wall. She looked up at the clock. Then she looked from side to side. No other swimmers were close.

Ledecky's time of 8:04.79 was a new world record for the event. She had

Katie Ledecky was already a highly decorated swimmer before the 2016 Olympics.

beaten the silver medalist by an amazing 11 seconds.

Ledecky is one of the best swimmers in history. The Maryland native has won individual Olympic and world titles in distances from 200 to 1,500 meters. No woman in history has posted faster times in the 400-, 800-, and 1,500-meter freestyle.

Thousands of female swimmers before her made Ledecky's excellence possible. Women were not always respected as athletes. The men who controlled sports didn't believe women should compete. Pioneers in the sport such as Annette Kellerman cleared the way so Ledecky and her peers could become stars today.

Annette Kellerman helped change the way female swimmers dressed when they competed.

Esther Williams became a film actress after her swimming career ended.

Kellerman was one of the first swimming pioneers. In the early 1900s, women had to wear baggy swimsuits made of wool. Kellerman pushed against these expectations. The Australian swimmer wore tighter suits. They looked more like the full-body swimsuits men wore. People were shocked that she didn't cover her shoulders and legs. But Kellerman's suits made it easier for her to swim.

Over time, women became more accepted in swimming. This brought more opportunities in the pool. Dawn Fraser was one of the sport's first big stars. The Australian broke records in the 100-meter freestyle race nine times between 1956 and 1964. Her final record time remained

BIG SPLASH IN HOLLYWOOD

US swimmer Esther Williams set the 100-meter breaststroke record in 1939. She qualified for the 1940 Olympics. But the Games were canceled due to World War II (1939–45). Instead, Williams decided to perform with aquatic shows. She was discovered by a Hollywood talent scout and had a long career as a movie actress.

the standard for eight years. That's a long time for a record to stand in swimming.

Before the 1964 Summer Olympics, Fraser was in a serious car crash. She was injured, and her mother was killed. But Fraser fought back to qualify for her third Olympic Games. There she won gold in the 100-meter freestyle. That made her the first swimmer to win gold in the same event at three Olympic Games. In total, she won eight medals, four of them gold.

Dawn Fraser shows off her gold medal that she won in the 100-meter freestyle at the 1964 Summer Olympics in Tokyo, Japan.

CHAPTER 2

OPEN-WATER LEGENDS

Some of the most famous swimmers weren't racing to beat an opponent. Instead they were trying to swim long distances across open water. The English Channel separates France and England. A man became the first person to swim the English Channel in 1875. At that time, women were thought to be too weak to swim that long distance. But 51 years later, Gertrude Ederle shocked the world.

In 1926, Ederle swam 35 miles (56 km) from France to England. She completed

Gertrude Ederle made a name for herself in the English Channel.

it in 14 hours, 31 minutes. That smashed the men's record time by nearly two hours.

Ederle was already a well-known swimmer. She had won a gold medal at the 1924 Olympic Games. Ederle's swimming accomplishments were honored in 1965. She was inducted into the International Swimming Hall of Fame.

Open-water, long-distance swims continue to draw people from all over the world. Natalie du Toit is a competitive swimmer from South Africa. She began racing internationally when she was only 14. When she was 17, she was in a car accident. She lost one of her legs. But that did not stop her from swimming.

In 2004, du Toit competed in the Paralympic Games. She won five gold medals at the Games. Then in 2008, she qualified for the Olympic Games in the open-water event. Du Toit was the

Paralympic gold medalist Natalie du Toit also competed in the Olympic Games.

first amputee to compete against non-disabled swimmers at the Games. Du Toit did not medal in the 10-kilometer race. But she proved athletes of all abilities can compete alongside one another. Du Toit retired from swimming after winning three more gold medals and one silver at the 2012 Paralympic Games.

Diana Nyad walks to the shore after completing her swim from Cuba to Florida in 2013.

Open-water swims are dangerous for many reasons. The distance is only one of them. Sharks are another. Most swimmers use a shark cage for safety. But Diana Nyad wanted to complete a swim without the cage's protection. Nyad knew she could swim the 110 miles (177 km) from Cuba to Florida. Attempts in 2011 and 2012 failed. But Nyad wasn't ready to give up.

In 2013, at age 64, she set out again. After more than 52 hours in the water without a shark cage, Nyad reached Key West, Florida. She was sunburned. Her lips and face were swollen from the saltwater. She was exhausted. But as she walked onto the beach in Florida, she pumped her fist in the air. Nyad did what others thought was impossible.

QUEEN OF THE CHANNEL

Alison Streeter is a swimmer from the United Kingdom. She holds the record for the most crossings of the English Channel. As of 2020, she had done it 43 times. Her record earned her the nickname "Queen of the Channel."

Dara Torres celebrates after setting a US record in the 50-meter freestyle in 2008.

an Olympic medal. In total, Brigitha won 11 individual medals between Olympic, European, and World Championships.

Brigitha was one of many women to push boundaries in the pool. Dara Torres was a swimmer who never seemed to stop. The Californian competed at her first Olympics in 1984. Twenty-four years later, she was still going strong. Torres won three silver medals at the 2008 Olympics. She was 41 years old. That made her the oldest medalist ever in Olympic swimming. Torres was also the first swimmer to represent the United States at five Olympic Games. She ended her career with 12 Olympic medals, including four golds.

Janet Evans got an early start on her path to stardom. Evans finished her first race when she was four years old. By age 15 she was elite. Evans set three

KID BACKSTROKE

In 1988, Hungarian Krisztina Egerszegi became the youngest swimmer to win a gold medal at the Olympics. She was only 14 years old at the time. Egerszegi went on to compete in two more Olympic Games. Her specialty was the 200-meter backstroke. She won gold in all three Games she competed in. Egerszegi became only the second person in history to do that. The first was Dawn Fraser.

world records in 1987. And she was only getting started. The following year, Evans competed in the 1988 Summer Olympic Games. She won three gold medals and set another world record and an Olympic record in the process.

Another young US swimmer was the breakout star at the 2012 Olympics. At just 17 years old, Missy Franklin won five medals. Four of them were gold. Four years later she won another gold medal. Both of Franklin's individual gold medals in 2012 were in her signature stroke, the backstroke. She set a world record in the 200-meter event.

Janet Evans takes a break while training at the 1988 Summer Games in Seoul, South Korea.

CHAPTER 4

MODERN OLYMPIC STARS

Few athletes made as big of a splash at the 2016 Olympics as Simone Manuel. The Texan specializes in shorter freestyle races. In 2016, she took to the block in the 100-meter freestyle final. At the buzzer, the swimmers were off.

The race was close. But Manuel was not in the lead at first. Manuel fought back in the last 50 meters. Stroke by stroke, Manuel surged ahead. She gained on the competitors in the other lanes. Her arms reached out in one final push.

Simone Manuel waves to her fans before accepting one of her two gold medals at the 2016 Olympics.

Manuel touched the wall at the same time as Canadian swimmer Penny Oleksiak. They were the first swimmers to reach the wall. Because of the tie, they each won a gold medal.

Manuel's win was even more historic. She was the first Black woman from the United States to win an individual gold medal in swimming. And she wasn't done yet. With another gold and two silver medals, Manuel proved she was one of the world's fastest swimmers.

Lilly King is a US swimmer. The Indiana native specializes in the breaststroke. King competed in the 2016 Olympics in Rio when she was only 19 years old. The young swimmer gained the most attention for her outspoken manner.

As a kid, King learned to be confident. She wasn't afraid to speak up when she thought

Lilly King shows off her gold medal in the 100-meter breaststroke at the 2016 Olympics.

something was wrong. When she believed another athlete cheated to get to the 2016 Olympics, she said so. Then King went out and won the race anyway.

Jessica Long was born with serious health problems. Doctors had to amputate both of her legs below the knee when she was 18 months old. But that never seemed to slow Long down.

She began swimming when she was seven years old. In 2004, she made her Paralympic debut. She was just 12 years old when she represented the United States in Athens, Greece. There, she won three gold medals.

Twelve years later, Long won six more medals at the 2016 Paralympics. And she's still going strong. Through 2020, the Maryland native had won 23 Paralympic medals. Thirteen were gold.

SARAH SJÖSTRÖM

Sarah Sjöström set a world record in the 100-meter butterfly at the 2016 Olympics. But Sjöström didn't stop at the Olympics. As of 2020, Sjöström had won 16 individual World Championship medals. That was more than any woman in history.

Jessica Long prepares for a race at the 2012 Paralympics in London, England.

Female swimmers have been pushing the limits for more than a century. With Manuel, King, Ledecky, Long, and others leading the way, the sport's future is as bright as ever.

MILESTONES

1920
Ethelda Bleibtrey sets two world records in three events at the 1920 Olympic Games.

1926
Gertrude Ederle is the first woman to swim the English Channel.

1964
Dawn Fraser becomes the first swimmer to win the same event at three Olympic Games.

1976
Enith Brigitha is the first swimmer of African heritage to win an Olympic medal.

2008
At age 41, Dara Torres becomes the oldest Olympic medalist in swimming.

2016
Katie Ledecky breaks a world record and wins gold in the 800-meter freestyle finals at the Olympic Games.

GLOSSARY

amputee
A person who has lost an arm or a leg.

heritage
A person's family background.

inducted
Admitted into an honored position.

international
Outside of one's home country.

pioneer
A person who does things others have not done before.

TO LEARN MORE

To learn more about legendary women in swimming, go to **pressboxbooks.com/AllAccess**. These links are routinely monitored and updated to provide the most current information available.

INDEX